This book belongs to

....

I MOVE A LOT
AND THAT'S OKAY!

SHERMAINE PERRY-KNIGHTS

Dedication

This book is dedicated to you, the military child.
Your thoughts, feelings, and experiences are important.
You support each other, form strong friendships across
cultures, and make the best out of every new station
in any part of the world.

I move a lot, and I don't know if I'm okay with that. I'm a military brat. That is what they call us but I don't like that name.

I'm just Grace. I'm seven years old. I usually tell people, "As long as you don't call me brat, I'm okay with that."

Our family is just my mom, my dad, and me. Our house is yellow and green with a pointy roof. We are stationed at Fort Benning. It's the name of a military base in Columbus, Georgia.

Military families call it being "stationed," not living somewhere.
Stations change all the time. We moved here one year ago, and I have
a lot of friends.

Dad always calls being stationed a new adventure,
and I'm okay with that.

My dad is a soldier in the Army. Today he came home early from work. My dad hugged and kissed me on the forehead, like he always does. Something was different. Dad said that it was time for an adventure because he has orders. Military orders are important chores or rules given by the big boss to service members. You have to do what the big boss says to do. "No whining at all, and you can't say no!" Soldiers like me listen and follow directions, and that's okay.

Dad said we are moving to Italia *[ee-tah-lyah]*. That's how the Italians say "Italy." The Army needs us to go there. I heard that it is beautiful and has lots of beaches to play on.

As long as I can play on the beaches and swim, I'm okay with it.

I have lots of money in a really big water bottle. It's a different kind of piggy bank. I think I'm rich because the bottle is full.

Dad said the money is different where we are going, and I can exchange it when we get there.

The money in Italy is called euros. I have to remember to call them euros, not dollars.

As long as I am still rich, I'm okay with that.

I'm getting used to the idea of moving again. Today is a big day. The movers are here, and I feel really sad. Every time we go on a new adventure, something of mine gets lost or broken.

I want to stay home to help mom put our stuff in boxes, but I have to go to school.

Mom promised that I could put three toys in my backpack. So I chose Kody, my purple stegosaurus, my board game, and my jump rope.

I put my new skateboard next to them. I grabbed four toys, just in case mom lets me have four.

As long as I have Kody, I'm okay.

Looks like we will live out of a suitcase again. So I will wear the same few outfits. This time is cool because I get my own suitcase. I put lots of stickers on it so everybody knows it's mine.

As long as I can pull it through the airport like the grown-ups, that's okay.

My room is empty, and I feel sad. We are moving into the hotel on base. We call it TLF, and that means "temporary lodging facility."

There are three reasons why you have to live in a TLF as a kid. One, you just moved to a new place. Two, you are about to move out of a place. Three, something happened to your family's house.

TLF is brown and really long. It's our house for now until we get to Italy. Everyone uses the same kitchen to cook and wash dishes. My room is the last one at the end of the hall.

This place does not smell like my house, and that's okay.

Dad and I walk up and down the stairs. We did not see anyone, but that is normal. So we knock on a few doors, run and hide to see if anyone would come out. It's a fun game dad and I play.

I always laugh because dad picks me up and runs fast every time; this time, no room doors open. We are having fun, and that's okay.

We walk back to the room. Mom is not here. I wonder where is she?
Dad says mom went to grab a pizza. We always have pizza before a
new adventure. It always makes me smile. Pizza feels like home.

As long as we have pizza,
        I'm okay with that.

Mom says it's our job to help Dad on this new adventure. The Army needs me to be tough and to learn new things quickly when we PCS.

"PCS" is what the military calls a permanent change of station. It means that it is time for the family to move. When I hear PCS, I know it's time to leave our home and move again.

I'm a soldier too. A tiny soldier in the Army. I am tough, but all I can think about is how much I already miss this place.

If this new adventure is fun, that's okay.

Today is my going-away party. It is my last day at school, and I'm sad. We are moving in the middle of the school year. I really like my classmates and my teacher, Mr. Mossburg. They are really nice to me.

Mr. Mossburg says I can write letters to him, and he will read them to the class. My mom has the school address and my teacher's first name, because I don't know it.

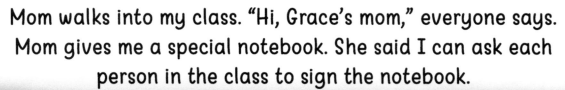

Mom walks into my class. "Hi, Grace's mom," everyone says. Mom gives me a special notebook. She said I can ask each person in the class to sign the notebook.

I really want to remember everyone. Sometimes when we move I forget people, and that makes me sad. As long as I can write letters to my class, that's okay.

My best friend, Kerrington, is not in my class.
She cannot come to my going-away party.
I hope I see her before we move to Italy.

I usually ride my bike to school. The movers are packing my bike, so Dad
is picking me up from school. He says there is a surprise waiting for me
in our room. The ride home is the longest ten-minute ride of my life.

I run to our room door. Mom opens it before I knock. Kerrington, her dad and mom were sitting at the table. I ask her to sign my notebook. I don't want to forget Kerrington. She was my first friend here and my best friend for now. Dad says we can play outside because the hotel has a playground. As long as there is a slide, I'm okay with it.

Today is another big day. Mom says our flight leaves tonight at ten o'clock. I get to stay up past my eight o'clock bedtime, and that's okay with me. Dad calls a taxi to take us to the airport. I hear a loud honk, and Mom yells, "It's here. The cab is here." So I walk outside with my suitcase dragging behind. I wave goodbye for the last time.

Traffic is really slow, and we are late. Dad says we had to get to the gate quickly. Mom holds my hand and pays the taxi driver. I know I'm getting too old to hold Mom's hand. I still like holding Mom's and Dad's hands, and that's okay.

The airport was busy, but the nice lady says we can go to the front of the line. Military families sometimes get to go to the front because we are soldiers. This time we get to ride on a cool cart all the way to the gate.

The plane is big and cold. I tell mom that I am scared. Mom says that she is scared too and we have to be brave. The Army needs us. I hug Kody and put on my seat belt. Dad covers me with a blanket. My ears are popping. Mom gives me watermelon-flavored bubble gum.

Dad said it is fourteen hours of flying. I keep wondering if we are there yet. My back hurts a little, so I use Kody as my personal pillow. He makes me feel good.

Kody feels like home, and I'm okay with that.

We're finally in Italy after a really long time. I see our bags, but I don't see Kody. I think I left him on the plane by accident. I feel so sad. Dad says he will buy me another dinosaur. I want Kody, not some imposter. Kody is going on an adventure without me, and that's not okay.

Everything I see looks so nice. Italy is beautiful. It's really hot outside and smells different. Dad says that there is sulfur in the air from volcanoes. What if one erupts while we are here? I can't believe Italy has volcanoes, and I'm not okay with that.

I roll down the window to smell the sulfur again. I'll have to get used to that. I don't know what the taxi driver is saying, but I like learning new things, so I'm okay with that.

Mom says the time in Italy is six hours ahead of the time in Fort Benning. It is like we are in the future. I will make sure to write that in my first letter to my old class. We are back at a hotel again. This hotel looks just like the one I left behind. It does not feel like home yet. I'm still waiting for my bed and toys to get here. Mom said it takes a few months for our stuff to get here.

As long as my toys get here soon, I'm okay with that.

We do not have a car yet. Dad says it will arrive by boat, and we can pick it up when it gets here. Until then, we are walking everywhere.

I wonder how much ice cream costs. I wonder if it tastes good. As long as I can still get some ice cream, then I'm okay with that.

I am taking a walk with Mom and smell something really good. I smile and ask Mom if we can go in there. I point to a store. Italians call it a pizzeria. I jump up and down and scream, "Pizza!" I wonder how much it costs. "Can I please have some, Mom?" "Yes, you can have some, but you have to ask how much in Italian. Remember how I taught you?"

I breathe deeply and point. "Scusi, quanto costa?"

[*SKOO-zi Kwon-toe COE-stah*] That's how you say, "Excuse me, how much?" in Italian. Mom pays the gentleman five euros. I watch the pizza man make the pizza right in front of us. I see him put it in the brick oven. This pizza is different but good, and I'm okay with that.

Today we are walking to my new school. I rush to the bathroom to comb my hair and put on my favorite dress and sneakers. I really don't know what to expect, and that's okay.

Mom says I start school next week at Naples Elementary School. It's white with a green, pointy roof, like my old school. There are so many kids here. So many faces that I don't know. Our mascot is a dolphin.

Since I love dolphins, I'm   with that.

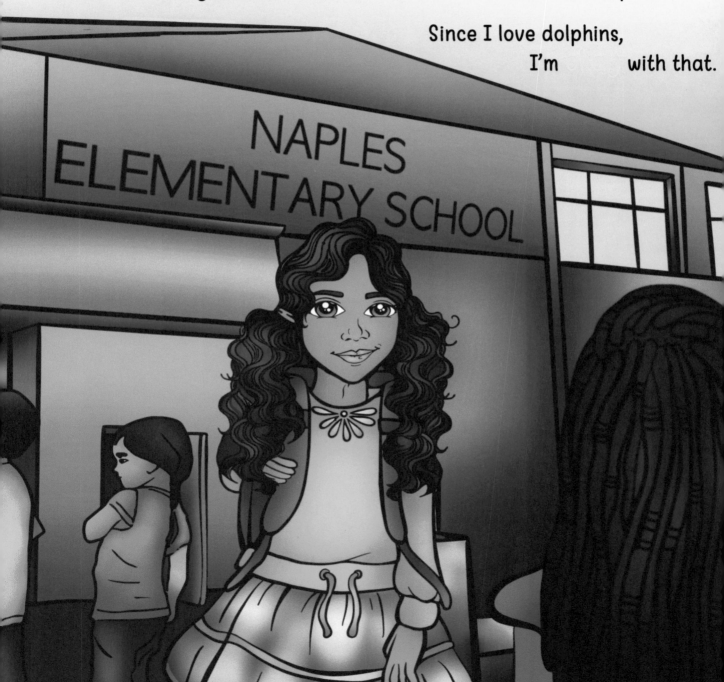

We are meeting our sponsor, Mr. Joe. A sponsor is a friendly face that greets you and your family at your new location and is a grown-up who knows the new place really well. Mr. Joe says he will make this adventure fun in Naples.

Today is another big day and Mr. Joe is helping us. We are moving into our new house. It is in a place called Castel Volturno *[ka'stel vol-turn-o]* near the water and we have a lake in our backyard. I'm so excited because I want to see my new room. I miss my toys. I miss my bike.

This time the movers are bringing boxes inside, and I can't understand what they are saying. I know only few words in Italian.

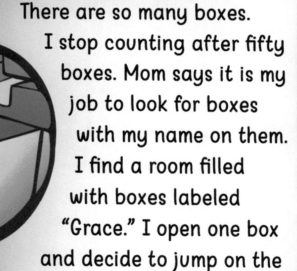

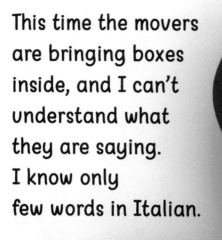

There are so many boxes. I stop counting after fifty boxes. Mom says it is my job to look for boxes with my name on them. I find a room filled with boxes labeled "Grace." I open one box and decide to jump on the bubble wrap.

Jumping on bubble wrap is one of the best parts of moving, and I'm okay with that.

This move is a tough one, but I'm a tough soldier. I want to tell my class all about Italy and what I've learned so far. I want to write a letter.

First, I'm going outside to play.

"Ciao *[Chaw]*, I'm Silvia. I live across the street," said a young girl. "What's your name?"

"Hi, io sono *[ee-oo so-no]* Grace. I move a lot, and I'm okay with that."

ABOUT THE AUTHOR

Shermaine Perry-Knights is an award-winning facilitator, project manager, and author. She facilitates coaching sessions, team-building sessions, and career readiness workshops. As a certified Associate Professional in Talent Development, Shermaine is passionate about helping others develop emotional intelligence and leadership skills.

Shermaine is a proud military kid and life-long learner. She earned a bachelor's of arts in political science from Spelman College and a master's in public administration from Strayer University. Shermaine has traveled throughout Asia and the West Indies, and she lived and studied in Europe and the Middle East.

As a master instructional designer, she is knowledgeable about learning development and facilitation of outcome-based learning programs. Shermaine Perry-Knights is recognized by the Association for Talent Development as the 2020 One To Watch.

Each of her published books support self-care, resilience, and career readiness. Explore those guided journals and adult coloring books on Amazon.com. You are invited to connect with Shermaine on instagram and facebook using the links below.

https://www.facebook.com/amazinglyshermaine
https://www.instagram.com/amazinglyshermaine/

Go to **www.innovationconsultants.co** for more information
on her educational consulting services.

CPSIA information can be obtained
at www.ICGtesting.com
Printed in the USA
LVHW072317260122
709481LV00002B/8